¡Baila Zambito!

Zenaida Ambukka

Balboa Press books may be ordered through booksellers or by contacting:

Balboa Press
A Division of Hay House
1663 Liberty Drive
Bloomington, IN 47403
www.balboapress.com
844-682-1282

ISBN: 978-1-9822-4850-5 (sc)
ISBN: 978-1-9822-4849-9 (e)

Print information available on the last page.

Balboa Press rev. date: 11/09/2020

BALBOA.PRESS
A DIVISION OF HAY HOUSE

Dedicado a mi niñito favorito, de tu abuelita Mimi. Eres el rey de mi corazón.

Dedicated to my favorite little boy, from your grandma Mimi. You are the king of my heart.

Mi nombre es Jeremías.

My name is Jeremiah.

Yo soy zambito claro.

I am light skinned, black and Hispanic.

Amo a mamá y papá.

I love mommy and daddy.

Y mis abuelas: Mimi...

And my grandma's Mimi...

y Glam-ma!

and Glam-ma!

También estoy mimado por mis madrinas: Jeana...

I am also spoiled by my godmothers: Jeana...

y Rebecca!

and Rebecca!

Me encanta jugar con la lana.

I love to play with yarn.

Me encanta patrullar en mi coche de policía.

I love to patrol around in my police car.

¿Sabes qué más? ¡Me encanta estar disfrazado!

Do you know what else? I love to be in disguise!

Pero más que nada... ¡Me encanta bailar!

But more than anything...I love to dance!

¡Mi abuela Mimi me dijo que soy Afro-Latino, descendiente del esclavo y que me muevo al ritmo del tambor Africano!

My grandma Mimi told me that I am Afro-Latino, descendant of the slave and that I move to the beat of the African drum!

Mi familia es originalmente de Kenya, Africa.

My family is originally from Kenya, Africa.

Hace un montón de tiempo, muchos esclavos fueron llevados a América Latina. Yo tengo familia en Perú y Cuba. ¡Incluso, hasta tengo familia en El Salvador!

A really long time ago, many slaves were taken to Latin America. I have family in Peru and Cuba. I even have family in El Salvador!

Vengo de una larga linaje de reyes y reinas.

I come from a long line of kings and queens.

¡Bailo con orgullo con mi gente, con mis amigos y con mi mamá!

I dance proudly with my people, with my friends and with my mom!

Bailamos al ritmo del tambor Africano.

We dance to the beat of the African drum.

¡La mayoría de la gente no puede seguir el ritmo de mis increíbles movimientos de baile!

Most people cannot keep up with my incredible dance moves!

Por parte de mi padre, tengo familia de Irlanda...

On my dad's side, I have family from Ireland...

... y creo que ahí es donde obtengo parte de mi técnica!

...and I think that's where I get part of my technique!

En Perú bailamos Festejo.

In Peru, we dance Festejo.

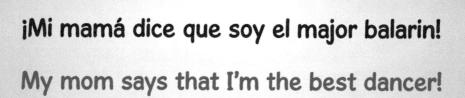

¡Mi mamá dice que soy el major balarín!

My mom says that I'm the best dancer!

¡Y si mi mamá lo dice, entonces debe ser verdad!

And if my mom says so, then it must be true!

El Fin.

The End.

About the Author

A proud Afro-Latina woman sharing stories inspired by her vibrant culture and her life as a loving mother and doting grandmother. Zenaida Ambukka is a woman who has suffered much prejudice from both the African American and Latino population. Growing up, she was often "too black" to fit in with other Latinos, and "too Hispanic" to fit in with the blacks. She also dealt with a great deal of colorism in her family life and was encouraged to marry outside her race "para mejorar la raza," ("better the race'") in the hopes that her children would have "good hair" and less prominent African features. Today, she stands strong and has love and acceptance for herself as an Afro-Latino woman and has since passed this love down to her beautiful daughter Morelia. Her mission is to bestow this same love to her adorable grandson Jeremiah (Jeremías), so that he may find pride and confidence at an early age in who he is as an Afro-Latino boy. She is making it her business to inform little Jeremiah & every little boy and girl like him, that Africa, too is their motherland and that "light skinned" or "dark", their ethnicity as a Latino does not make them any "less black."